ANIMAL TRACKERS
AROUND THE WORLD

DOWN UNDER

Tessa Paul

CRABTREE
Publishing Company

350 Fifth Avenue	360 York Road, R.R.4	73 Lime Walk
Suite 3308	Niagara-on-the-Lake	Headington, Oxford
New York, NY 10118	Ontario LOS IJO	England OX3 7AD

Editor **Greg Nickles**
Designer **Janelle Barker**
Consultant **Karen Jane Kemmis-Betty (M.Sc.)**

Illustrations
Andrew Beckett (cover background, track marks)
All other illustrations courtesy of Marshall Cavendish Partworks: Evi Antoniou (pages 4-5, 6); Andrew Beckett
(pages 4-5, 14, 15, 20, 21, 26-27); Wendy Bramail (page 19); Robin Budden/WLAA (page 11); Mike
Donnelly/WLAA (pages 4-5, 12); Ruth Grewcock (page 19); Steve Kingston (page 31); Rachel Lockwood/WLAA
(page 30); Alan Male/Linden Artists (page 29); John Morris/WLAA (page 17); Andie Peck/WLAA (page 23);
Nike Pike/WLAA (pages 22, 25); Peter David Scott/WLAA (pages 7, 13); Chris Shields/WLAA (pages 10-11);
Guy Troughton (pages 16, 24); Simon Turvey/WLAA (pages 4-5, 8-9, 18, 28)

First printed 1998
Copyright © 1998 Crabtree Publishing Company

Cataloging-in-Publication Data

Paul, Tessa

Down under / Tessa Paul
p. cm — (Animal trackers)
Includes index.
ISBN 0-86505-588-2 (library bound)   ISBN 0-86505-596-3 (pbk.)
Summary: Introduces the physical characteristics, behavior, and tracks of a variety of animals
that live in or around Australia, including the platypus, kiwi, and Tasmanian devil.
1. Zoology—Australia—Juvenile literature. [1. Zoology—Australia. 2. Animal tracks.]
I. Title. II. Series: Paul, Tessa. Animal trackers.
QL338.P345 1998   j591.994   LC 98-2561
CIP

CONTENTS

DOWN UNDER

If you look at a
globe of the world,
you will find
the continent
of Australia
hidden under the lower curve.
Nearby, you will see the islands of New
Zealand and New Guinea. These places are
said to be "down under" because of where
they are found
on the globe.

The animals found
in these lands are
very different from
those in other places.

Koalas look like bears, but are not. There are birds that cannot fly. The kangaroo hops on its two hind legs. The platypus has a ducklike bill, digs burrows, and oozes milk from its belly!

There are many interesting animals "down under." In this book, you will meet some of these unusual creatures including marsupials, or animals that carry and suckle their young in a pouch, and monotremes, the only mammals that lay eggs.

PLATYPUS

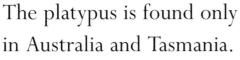
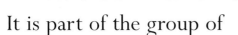

The platypus is found only in Australia and Tasmania. It is part of the group of mammals called monotremes. Monotremes are the only mammals that lay eggs. Platypuses live in, or near, water. They dig their burrows in the banks of freshwater rivers and lakes.

QUICK DRY
After it has been in the water, the platypus slips into its burrow. It will come out with its fur dry and glossy. The sides of the burrow help squeeze dry the thick coat.

SNAIL   **CRAYFISH**

SHRIMP   **TADPOLE**

PLATYPUS PREY
A platypus has no teeth. Horny ridges in its jaws, bill, and mouth help grind its food.

WEBBED FEET
Platypuses have webbed feet. They pull this webbing back when they are on land.

A USEFUL BILL

A platypus cannot see or hear underwater because it closes its eyes and ears when diving. Its bill, however, can sense objects, such as rocks, in the river. With its bill, the platypus scoops up food from the river bed. The food is stored in cheek pouches. A dive lasts for about a minute.

DIVING GEAR

During a dive, the platypus uses its front legs to help it swim. Beneath its short, thick fur is an undercoat that keeps the platypus warm in cold water.

Platypuses live in burrows that form a maze of tunnels. The platypus mating season starts in midwinter. In Australia, winter falls between July and October. Platypuses have a playful mating ritual. The female goes looking for a male. When she meets one, he grasps her tail and, together, they swim around in circles. Three or four days after mating, the female begins to prepare her breeding burrow.

A LONG NEST

A female platypus digs a breeding burrow that is 39 to 49 feet (twelve to fifteen meters) long. A chamber is at the end. She lines it with leaves. To keep other animals out, she bars the entrance with wet leaves, grass, and walls of mud. Within a month after mating, the female lays two eggs in the chamber.

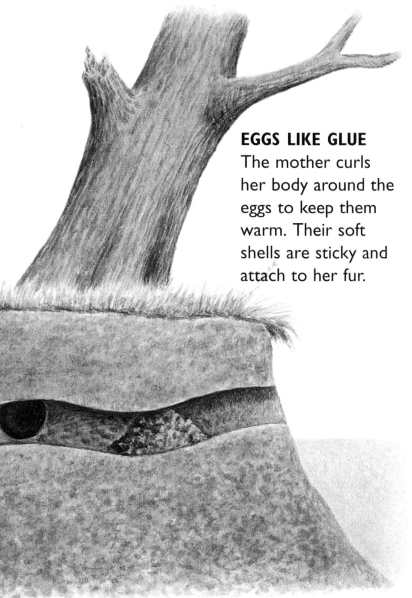

EGGS LIKE GLUE

The mother curls her body around the eggs to keep them warm. Their soft shells are sticky and attach to her fur.

EGG AND MILK

While inside their egg, baby platypuses grow a sharp little tooth. It is used to cut through their egg shell. The young are half-an-inch (thirteen millimeters) long when they are born. They have no lips or bill. Their mother has no nipples. Her milk oozes from a glandular patch on her under-belly. The young lick up the milk.

SWIMMING LESSONS

When the young platypuses are about six months old, they stop feeding from their mother. By this time, they have a beak and fur. The mother leads them from the burrow to take their first swim. The young stay with the mother until they are about a year old. Fathers do not help care for the young platypuses.

DINGO

Dingoes are wild dogs found
in Australia. They were brought
to Australia by people about
4,000 years ago. The dogs turned
wild and roamed all over the
continent. Today, farmers think
dingoes are pests because they
raid flocks of sheep. A fence over
3,000 miles (4 800 kilometers)
long was built to control the
dingoes. It protects much
of eastern Australia by forcing
the dingoes to live in
remote, harsh parts
of the land.

BACK TO FRONT
Dingo tracks are the same
as those of other large dogs.
When dingoes run, their
hind feet touch the ground
before their front feet.

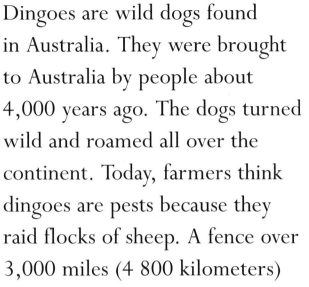
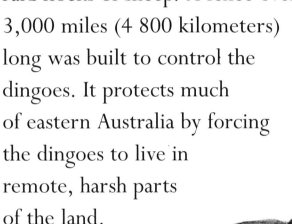

FAMILY HELP

A mother dingo stays close to her babies during their first month of life. The father brings food to her. Then both parents hunt for food, and the cubs learn to eat meat. The mother may give birth to another litter within the year. The older cubs help look after the babies.

FAMILY AND FRIENDS

Dingoes live in families. A dingo family is led by a pair of dingoes. They are called the "alpha" male and female. Their young live with them for two or three years. Sometimes a family joins others to form a pack. They do this to hunt large animals, such as the kangaroo. Dingoes usually eat small mammals, such as wombats and rabbits.

11

ECHIDNA

Echidnas, like platypuses, are monotremes. There are two species of echidnas. Short-beaked echidnas live in Australia, Tasmania, and New Guinea. Long-beaked echidnas are found only in New Guinea. Both kinds are active when the weather is cool, so they usually come out at night. When they are alarmed, they quickly dig a hole, then roll into a ball and hide inside the hole.

HEAVY CLAWS

Echidnas walk with their legs held straight. These are the tracks of the short-beaked echidna. Its hind claws leave deep marks in the ground.

SOME DIFFERENCES

The long-beaked echidna is bigger than its Australian cousin. Both are covered with coarse hairs and have sharp spines on their back. Short-beaked echidnas have four claws on their front and back feet. Long-beaked echidnas have only three claws on each hind foot. The claws are used for grooming and digging.

HOOKS AND GLUE

Echidnas have a tiny mouth
at the end of their snout. They
use their tongue to catch food.
Short-beaked echidnas eat termites
and ants. They catch them on the
sticky surface of their long tongue.
Long-beaked echidnas have
a tongue covered with
small hooks, which
trap worms.

DIG AND GRIND

A short-beaked echidna uses
its keen sense of smell to find
ants. It digs at earth and logs with
its claws. Its long snout is strong
and pushes through loose earth.
Its tongue shoots out to catch
the ants. Echidnas have no
teeth, but hard ridges
in their mouth grind
up the food.

KIWI

Kiwis are found only in New Zealand. They are named for their shrill cry: "ki-wi." They belong to a group of birds called ratites. This name means that they do not fly. Kiwis' wings are just stubs. Their plumage is loose and hair-like. Kiwis eat fruit and insects, so they prefer to live in forests, where it is easy to find food. They have, however, learned to survive in open areas.

EGG DIET

Kiwis dig nests hidden in bushes, or nest in a hollow log. A female lays one egg. The male sits on it for about 80 days before it hatches. At first, the newly hatched chick feeds off a yolk sac from the egg. After a week, it finds its own food.

A THIRD LEG

The kiwi has short legs and sharp claws. When standing, kiwis rest the tip of their beak on the ground. Sometimes they lean on it for support.

FOREST TRACK

A kiwi's thick toes and claws leave a clear print in the moist forest floor.

CATCHING FOOD

Kiwis use their bill to probe the forest floor for food. They thrust the bill deep into the earth. The food is picked up on the tip of the bill. Then, with quick, jerking actions, kiwis throw the food to the back of their throat.

NIGHT WAYS

Kiwis are nocturnal but cannot see in the dark. They find their way around with their sensitive nose and the bristles on their face.

15

KANGAROO

Kangaroos are marsupials. Marsupials are mammals that carry and suckle their young in a pouch. They are found in the Americas and Australia, but kangaroos are found only in Australia. They live in most parts of the continent, and are able to survive in many types of climate. They prefer to live near water, although they can go for a week without drinking.

SPRINGBOARD
The kangaroo has long, narrow hind feet that act like springboards when the animal leaps.

EATING POSES
Kangaroos stand to nibble at bushes and shrubs. When they stand or sit, kangaroos use their heavy tail for balancing. They eat at dawn and spend most of the day resting in shade.

FIGHTING TO MATE

Male kangaroos fight over the females.
The male that wins mates with many
females. After about 30 days,
a pregnant female gives birth to
a baby, or "joey," that is only
three-quarters-of-an-inch (two
centimeters) long. Just before her
baby is born, the mother licks her pouch
clean. The joey leaves the birth passage
and, without any help from its mother,
finds its way to the pouch and climbs in.

IN THE POUCH

Inside the kangaroo mother's
pouch, the joey attaches itself
to a teat. The teat swells in
the joey's mouth and provides
a constant supply of milk.
Joeys stay in the pouch for
about six months. Then they
stay with their mother until
they are about two years old.

WOMBAT

Wombats are marsupials found in Australia and Tasmania. They are squat, heavy animals that live in burrows. Wombats walk on the flats of their feet in the same way bears do. Their short, strong legs do not move fast, but are good for burrowing. Wombats also have strong claws to help dig through the earth. They are very timid, and spend much of their lives underground.

LOOKING BACK

A female wombat has a pouch that opens backwards to help shield her baby when the mother moves underground. It also stops earth from entering the pouch.

NEW TEETH

Wombats live in dry areas where bushes and thorny trees grow. They are herbivores, and eat grasses, shrubs, roots, leaves, or bark. They have a split upper lip. This lip parts to let their teeth clamp around the food. Their sharp teeth wear down, but grow and renew themselves often.

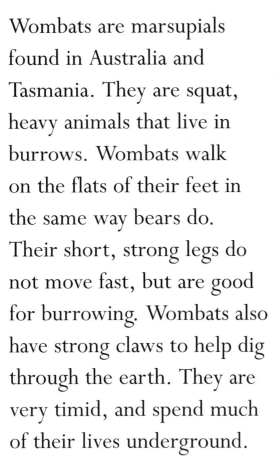

CATCHING THE SUN

Wombats dig shallow pits above their burrows. They lie in the pits and "sunbathe" in the warmth of the morning sun.

TUNNELING

Wombats use their front feet to dig. Hind feet kick the newly dug soil out of the burrow.

VISITORS ONLY

Wombats' burrows have tunnels and chambers. Wombats live alone, but visit each other. The young live with their mother. They leave her when they are almost two years old.

SOFT AND COSY

Wombats line their chambers with soft, dry leaves and grass. The plants make cosy bedding.

EMU

Emus are large, shaggy birds. They are ratites, and live in Australia. Emus eat flowers, fruit, leaves, insects, and lizards. They love to eat fresh plant growth, so they follow the rains in search of new plants. They drink water often. In parts of Australia where water is hard to find, emus raid farms to drink the livestock's water.

FOLLOWING FOOD

Emus have long legs, ending in three toes. They are hardy birds, and will walk great distances to find food. They run as fast as 30 miles per hour (48 kilometers per hour).

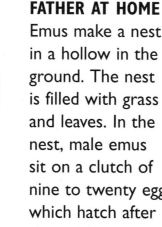

FATHER AT HOME

Emus make a nest in a hollow in the ground. The nest is filled with grass and leaves. In the nest, male emus sit on a clutch of nine to twenty eggs, which hatch after about 50 days.

FIERCE GUARD

Emu chicks are born with a thick, striped down. Their father stays with them for the first six months of their lives, but sometimes he stays longer. He guards his chicks so fiercely that he will even chase their mother away.

VOICES

Emus make many noises. They often gurgle and grunt. During courtship, the female gives out single, booming cries. This is called "drumming." The sounds are made through an air sac on the neck. It inflates when the female is drumming. Young emus make whistling sounds.

EMU WAYS

Emus are active during the day, and rest in the open at night. They are nomadic, which means they do not stay in one territory, but move around constantly. They are not easy to tame or farm because they are very aggressive.

KOALA

Koalas are marsupials. They are found all over Australia. They have dense, wooly fur and leathery noses. Each lives alone in its own tree. Baby koalas live with their mother for a year. Then they go off to find a tree of their own.

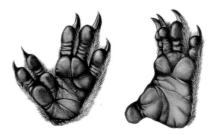

TIGHT GRIP
A koala's hand has two thumbs, which grip onto branches. The foot has one strong thumb. The claws on the feet and hands are used for climbing and grooming. The pads are rough.

A SAFE BERTH
A female koala is pregnant for about 30 days. The baby is very tiny and, at birth, heads straight for the pouch. It stays in the pouch for five months, feeding on its mother's milk.

BELLOWING BOY

Koalas are solitary, but
do form loose groups.
Mothers live with their young
and attack any others who come to
their tree. Koalas do, however, live close to
other koalas. One male often has six female
neighbors. In the mating season, the male leaves
a scent trail by rubbing his chest against the tree
trunks. He bellows loudly to frighten away other
males and to attract the females.

EASY LIVING

Koalas spend a lot of the day sleeping. Their digestive system works slowly, so koalas do not have much energy. They are most active after sunset.

MOTHER'S GIFT

A koala carries a kind of bacteria in its body. This helps it to digest its leafy diet. Mother koalas bring up some of their own food to feed their babies. In this way, they pass the bacteria into a baby's body.

Koalas eat only eucalyptus leaves. They will not eat other food. A koala chooses a eucalyptus tree and settles on it. It has no need to forage for food. It simply ambles along a branch and picks some leaves to eat.

FEW PRINTS

Koalas rarely leave their trees, so their tracks are not seen often. Koalas are quick but awkward on the ground. If a dingo or a fox attacks it, a koala lashes out with its claws.

A TASTE FOR EUCALYPTUS

Koalas have big back teeth that grind their food. Grinding takes a long time, so koalas store food in their cheeks while they grind a mouthful. Koalas do not eat just any kind of eucalyptus leaves. They develop a taste for one or two types. If they move to another tree, they check that the leaves have the "right" taste.

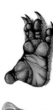

KOOKABURRA

GROUP SCREAM

Kookaburras are famous for their call, a loud, shrill "kook, kook, kook, ka-ka." Groups call and shout together at dawn and dusk.

SHORT AND FLESHY

Kookaburra feet are weak and fleshy. The second and third toes are partly joined. Their bodies are heavy and round, and their legs are very short.

Kookaburras are a kind of kingfisher found in Australia. They live in woods and trees near rivers and marshes. Kookaburras live in groups of a mating pair and one or two helpers. Their beak is long and makes a good weapon when the birds are hunting. Kookaburras eat insects, small birds, lizards, snakes, and small mammals.

HARD PLACES

Kookaburras nest in old logs or hollows in trees. They do not line their nests with leaves or twigs. In the nest, both parents sit on about six eggs. These hatch in about 30 days.

TAKING AIM

A kookaburra swoops down on a fish. It uses its bill to sieze the fish, then flies sharply upwards. Kookaburras can spot prey from a long way off. They are spectacular divers, and they are swift and accurate in their aim.

HELPERS

Kookaburras pair for life and share the duties of rearing their chicks. The young are fed by the adults for almost ten weeks after birth. The parents, however, have helpers at the nest. These helpers are other adult birds who hunt and bring food to the nestlings. The helpers also guard the nests.

BANDICOOT

Bandicoots are marsupials. They look like mice, but are the size of rabbits. They live in the forests and grasslands of Australia and New Guinea. Bandicoots eat insects. The wooded areas where they live have lots of this kind of food.

TWO INTO ONE

The bandicoot's second and third toes are joined together, and end in one claw. The claw is used for grooming. Bandicoots groom themselves often.

HUNTER AND PREY

Bandicoots hunt the insects of the forest floor. In turn, they are hunted by dingoes, foxes, and birds of prey, such as harrier hawks. When bandicoots are frightened, they give a shrill squeak. They jump straight up into the air, and then run off. Sometimes bandicoots huff and bare their teeth.

GARDEN DIGS

The bandicoot feeds at night. It pokes its long nose into roots to find food. Its claws dig the topsoil to uncover insects. People often find holes in their garden where bandicoots have fed.

LITTLE BEANS

Bandicoots have three or four young. A newborn is the size of a bean. It creeps into its mother's pouch and stays there for about 70 days. Soon after the young leave the pouch, they can start eating insects.

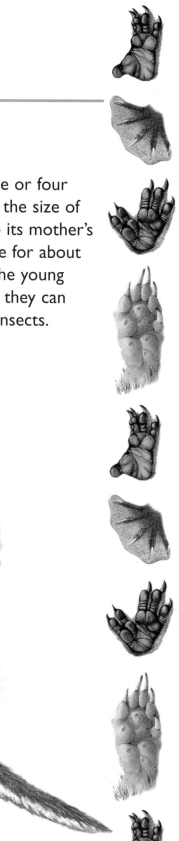

MY PLACE

Bandicoots stay in one small territory, which they guard carefully. Every night, the male checks that no other bandicoot has moved into his area. He also checks that his female neighbors are still nearby. Bandicoots do not have dens. For shelter, they shuffle into a pile of leaves. The pregnant females use a hollow in the ground as a nest.

TASMANIAN DEVIL

NO WASTE
When eating, a Tasmanian devil drags its food to a quiet place. Using its strong teeth and jawbones, the Tasmanian devil crushes and eats the skin, guts, muscles, and small bones of its prey.

The Tasmanian devil, found only in Tasmania, is a marsupial that eats meat. The name "devil" comes from the Tasmanian devil's growling call and the fact that the animal kills farmers' sheep and chickens.

FAMILY TIES
The male Tasmanian devil stays with the female during her pregnancy and when the infants are young. He defends and feeds the mother, but ignores his own babies. The female carries four babies in her pouch for about four months. They stay with her for about a year.

TASMANIAN DEVIL PREY
Although Tasmanian devils can be hunters, they are usually scavengers. This means they eat meat left behind by other animals.

WOMBAT   **POSSUM**   **LAMB**   **POULTRY**

BEAR-LIKE
The Tasmanian devil is the size of a small dog, but it has the sturdy shape of a bear. It often growls and snarls.

CLAWS IN ACTION
The Tasmanian devil's claws are not long, but it uses them to climb trees, dig holes, and drag around its food.

INDEX

GLOSSARY

Carnivore - An animal that eats mainly meat

Camouflage - Many animals have a coat or skin that blends with the color of the place where they live. This is called camouflage. Camouflage hides an animal from predators or from prey it is trying to catch.

Herbivore- An animal that feeds mainly on plants

Mammal – An animal that does not lay eggs but gives birth to its young. A mammal mother produces milk to feed her baby.

Marsupial - A mammal that carries and suckles its young in a pouch

Migrate - Animals migrate when they travel long distances for food, warmth, or to breed.

Monotreme - A mammal that lays eggs

Predator – An animal that hunts and eats other animals, called prey

Prey - An animal that is hunted by another animal, called a predator

Plumage - The feathers covering a bird

Ratite - A bird that cannot fly

1 2 3 4 5 6 7 8 9 0 Printed in the U.S.A. 7 6 5 4 3 2 1 0 9 8